37 Miracles of Jesus

I	Jesus Turns Water Into Wine
2	Jesus Heals an Official's Son
3	Jesus Casts Out an Evil Spirit
4	Jesus Heals Peter's Mother-in-Law
5	Healing the Sick and Oppressed
6	Miraculous Fish Catch on Lake Gennesaret
7	Jesus Heals a Man With Leprosy
8	Jesus Heals a Centurion's Paralyzed Servant
9	Jesus Heals a Paralytic
10	Jesus Heals Man with Withered Hand
11	Jesus Raises a Widow's Son from the Dead
12	Jesus Calms the Storm
13	Jesus Casts Demons into a Herd of Pigs
14	Jesus Heals a Woman in the Crowd
15	Jesus Raises Jairus' Daughter Back to Life
16	Jesus Heals Two Blind Men
17	Jesus Heals a Man Who Was Unable to Speak
18	Jesus Heals an Invalid at Bethesda
19	Jesus Feeds the Five Thousand
20	Jesus Walks on Water
21	Jesus Heals the Sick in Gennesaret
22	Jesus Heals Woman's Demon-Possessed Daughter
23	Jesus Heals a Deaf and Mute Man
24	Jesus Feeds the Four Thousand
25	Jesus Heals a Blind Man at Bethsaida
26	Jesus Heals a Man Born Blind
27	Jesus Heals a Demon-Possessed Boy
28	The Temple Tax
29	Jesus and Beelzebul
30	Jesus Heals Woman Crippled for 18 years
31	Jesus Heals a Man on the Sabbath
32	Jesus Heals Ten Men With Leprosy
33	Jesus Raises Lazarus from the Dead
34	Blind Bartimaeus Receives His Sight
35	The Withered Fig Tree
36	Jesus Heals a Servant's Severed Ear
37	The Second Miraculous Catch of Fish

Once upon a time, in a little town called Bethlehem, a very special baby was born. His name was Jesus, and even though he was a tiny baby, he was destined to change the world. Jesus was born in a simple stable, surrounded by gentle animals, because there was no room for his family in the inn. From the start, he was loved by people near and far, with shepherds and wise men traveling to see this miraculous child, guided by a shining star.

As Jesus grew up in Nazareth, he became known for his kindness and wisdom, always eager to help others. He was curious about everything and loved to share stories with those he met, teaching lessons of love and compassion. Jesus taught everyone about the importance of being good to one another, spreading messages of friendship and care. People soon realized that Jesus wasn't just an ordinary boy; he was someone with a big heart ready to inspire change in the world!

Jesus Turns Water Into Wine

In the village of Cana in Galilee, a wedding celebration is underway, marking a special occasion with joy and festivity. Jesus, his mother Mary, and his disciples are among the invited guests, blending into the jubilant milling of friends and family. However, the celebration faces an impending crisis: the wine runs out prematurely, which may result in social embarrassment for the hosts. Recognizing the situation, Mary approaches Jesus, hinting at the problem and offering him an opportunity to intervene in this unexpected shortage.

Initially, Jesus responds to Mary with a gentle reminder that his hour has not yet come, suggesting a divine timing for revealing his purpose. Nevertheless, Mary, with quiet confidence in her son's abilities, instructs the servants to follow Jesus' directions without question. Nearby, six stone water jars are used for Jewish purification rituals, each able to hold significant amounts of water. Jesus instructs the servants to fill these jars with water, and they comply, filling them to the brim—an act of simple obedience that sets the stage for an extraordinary transformation.

As the water is drawn from the jars and presented to the master of the banquet, it is revealed to have become exemplary wine. The master, unaware of the miracle that has occurred, is astounded by the quality and praises the groom for saving the best wine for last. This moment, discreet yet profound, marks the first miracle of Jesus, revealing his glory and deepening the faith of his disciples. The transformation of water into wine at Cana is not only an act of divine power but also a symbol of abundance and the new creation that characterizes Jesus' ministry, offering a glimpse into the transformative nature of his presence in the world.

Jesus Heals an Official's Son

After spending two days among the Samaritans, Jesus continues his journey to Galilee, where he is now welcomed by the Galileans who had witnessed his works during the feast in Jerusalem. This region is familiar territory, yet it harbors a complex reception of Jesus' ministry—a mix of hospitality and skepticism. Amidst this setting, an official from Capernaum, desperate and stricken with worry, approaches Jesus. His son is gravely ill, and the father's journey to Jesus is a testament to his desperation and flickering hope that Jesus can perform yet another miracle.

The official pleads with Jesus to come down and heal his dying son, illustrating a belief that hinges on Jesus' physical presence to effect healing. Jesus responds with a challenge, noting that many require signs and wonders to believe, indirectly addressing the broader demand for proof among the people. Nevertheless, sensing the official's urgent faith, Jesus offers a simple yet profound proclamation: "Go, your son will live." This phrase calls the official to trust not in what he can see, but in Jesus' word alone. The man takes Jesus at his word, setting off on his journey back home, embodying a transition from seeking signs to exercising faith.

While the official travels, his servants meet him with the joyous news that his son has recovered. Upon inquiring about the timing of the recovery, it becomes clear that it coincided precisely with the moment Jesus had declared his son would live. This revelation solidifies the man's belief, extending it to his entire household. The healing of the official's son is the second miraculous sign in John's Gospel, reinforcing the power of Jesus' word and fostering a deeper understanding of faith that transcends the need for physical evidence. This story serves as a powerful reminder of the potency of faith in Jesus' promises and the transformative impact such faith can have on individuals and their communities.

Jesus Casts Out an Evil Spirit

In the early days of his ministry, Jesus arrives in Capernaum and enters the synagogue on the Sabbath to teach, immediately captivating his audience. Unlike the scribes, Jesus teaches with unprecedented authority, a striking difference that leaves the congregation amazed. His words carry a weight and clarity that resonate deeply, prompting an attentive silence among those gathered. The synagogue, a center for learning and worship, becomes the setting for an unexpected demonstration of divine power that complements the authority of his teaching.

Amidst the teaching, a man possessed by an impure spirit abruptly interrupts, crying out in recognition and fear of Jesus' true identity. The spirit's confrontation reveals its awareness of Jesus as the Holy One of God, sparking tension within the sacred space. In a display of calm authority, Jesus rebukes the spirit, commanding it to be silent and to come out of the man. With convulsions and a loud shriek, the impure spirit obeys, leaving the man unharmed and freeing the congregation from the disruption. This miraculous exorcism reinforces the authoritative nature of Jesus' presence and teachings.

The congregation, witnessing both Jesus' authoritative teaching and the power of his command over the impure spirit, is left in awe and wonder. They question among themselves, marveling at this new teaching with authority that even unclean spirits obey. The event quickly spreads through the region, enhancing Jesus' reputation and drawing attention to his ministry. This account in Mark highlights the profound authority of Jesus—not only in words but also in actions—that validates his divine mission and signals the inbreaking of God's kingdom, offering liberation and new understanding to all who witness it.

Jesus Heals Peter's Mother-in-Law

After teaching in the synagogue at Capernaum, Jesus visits the home of Simon Peter. Upon entering, he is informed that Simon's mother-in-law is severely ill, suffering from a high fever. Her condition not only concerns her family but also affects the household's ability to function, especially in a culture where hospitality is highly regarded. Recognizing the urgency and impact of her illness, Jesus is moved with compassion and responds immediately to the need presented before him.

Approaching the bedside, Jesus bends over her, offering a gentle yet commanding presence that signifies both his concern and authority. He rebukes the fever, speaking directly to it as one would command an unwelcome guest. Instantly, the fever leaves her, and her recovery is so complete and immediate that she rises and begins to serve them. This act of service underscores the totality of her healing and highlights her gratitude and restored vitality. Jesus' intervention transforms the atmosphere of the home from one of distress to one of renewed hospitality and joy.

This healing miracle, though personal and domestic in scope, illustrates the reach and tenderness of Jesus' ministry. It demonstrates his power over illness and his desire to restore individuals to their communities and roles. The action not only alleviates the physical suffering of Simon's mother-in-law but also restores the normalcy and warmth of the home, allowing the family to extend hospitality once again. Through this account, Luke presents Jesus as a healer who brings holistic restoration, emphasizing the intimate and personalized nature of his compassion and authority.

Healing the Sick and Oppressed

As evening descends on Capernaum, the news of Jesus' healing power spreads quickly throughout the town. People begin to bring those who are sick or suffering from various diseases to him, forming a gathering around the house where Jesus stays. Each person carries a hope for relief and restoration, representing the diverse ailments and burdens afflicting the community. This scene reflects a collective yearning and faith in Jesus' ability to transform their circumstances, underscoring the impact of his earlier acts of healing.

Jesus, moved by compassion, takes the time to lay hands on each person, individually attending to their maladies. His personal touch serves as a symbol of his care and the power flowing from him, as each one experiences healing. This methodical and deliberate act showcases not only his divine authority but also the personal attention he affords to every suffering individual. As a result, a wave of health and freedom sweeps through the crowd, reinforcing the hope and faith they placed in him.

Among those healed are individuals possessed by demons, who, driven out by the presence of Jesus, acknowledge him as the Son of God. These declarations, however, are silenced by Jesus, who commands the spirits not to speak further. He exercises control not only over physical ailments but also over spiritual forces, demonstrating his authority over all aspects of human suffering. Through these healings, Jesus establishes his role as the Messiah with the power to restore wholeness, providing a glimpse of the kingdom of God breaking into the world through his ministry.

As Jesus stands by the shore of Lake Gennesaret, a large crowd presses in on him, eager to hear the word of God. He notices two boats at the water's edge, left there by fishermen who are washing their nets after a fruitless night. Jesus steps into Simon's boat and asks him to push out a little from the shore. From this vantage point, he continues teaching the crowd, turning the boat into a pulpit that enables him to address the growing multitude with clarity and authority. This setup reflects Jesus' innovative approach to reaching people, using everyday settings to communicate spiritual truths.

After his teaching, Jesus makes a seemingly unusual request to Simon, instructing him to "put out into the deep and let down the nets for a catch." Though Simon initially expresses doubt, noting their lack of success the previous night, he complies out of respect for Jesus. To their astonishment, the nets fill to breaking point with a tremendous catch of fish, so overwhelming that they signal their partners in the other boat for assistance. The boats become so laden that they begin to sink, demonstrating the superabundance that accompanies obedience to Jesus' word, even in seemingly mundane tasks.

Witnessing this miraculous catch, Simon Peter is overcome with awe and falls at Jesus' knees, confessing his own unworthiness and sinfulness, recognizing the divine power at work. Jesus reassures Simon, telling him not to be afraid, for from now on he will "catch people." This call signifies a transformation of vocation, as Simon, along with James and John, the sons of Zebedee, leaves everything behind to follow Jesus. This event illustrates the transition from an ordinary life to one of extraordinary purpose, as Jesus calls his first disciples to join him in his mission, marking the beginning of their journey as fishers of men in the kingdom of God.

Jesus Heals a Man With Leprosy

As Jesus descends from the mountainside, a large crowd follows him, captivated by his teaching and authority. Amidst the multitude, a man with leprosy approaches, breaking through the social barriers that typically isolate those with his condition. Lepers are considered unclean and are often marginalized, living on the outskirts of society. Yet, with a profound display of faith and desperation, this man kneels before Jesus, addressing him as "Lord" and expressing his belief in Jesus' power by saying, "If you are willing, you can make me clean." His approach is both an act of courage and a testament to the hope that Jesus inspires in outcasts.

In response, Jesus reaches out and touches the man, an action both compassionate and significant, as touching a leper is socially and religiously taboo. With the simple but profound declaration, "I am willing, be clean," Jesus heals the man instantly. The touch signifies not only the restoration of health but also the breaking down of barriers that have isolated the leper from his community. This moment underscores Jesus' willingness to engage personally and powerfully with those who are marginalized and suffering, demonstrating the inclusive and transformative nature of his ministry.

After healing the man, Jesus instructs him to show himself to the priest and offer the gift Moses commanded as a testimony. This directive serves as both a fulfillment of religious law and a public verification of the man's restoration to community life. By doing so, Jesus adheres to the cultural customs while simultaneously revealing his authority over illness and impurity. This healing narrative highlights Jesus' compassion and authority, illustrating the power and reach of his ministry as he restores individuals physically and socially, embodying the inbreaking of God's kingdom on earth.

Jesus Heals a Centurion's Paralyzed Servant

In the town of Capernaum, a Roman centurion approaches Jesus with an urgent plea. Breaking cultural norms and barriers, this officer of the occupying force shows humility and concern for a servant who is suffering tremendously from paralysis. Despite his authoritative position, the centurion comes to Jesus with respect and faith, demonstrating an unusual empathy and understanding. His appeal to Jesus reflects not only his desperation but also his deep belief in Jesus' power to heal beyond ethnic and social boundaries.

When Jesus offers to go to the centurion's home to heal the servant, the centurion displays a remarkable understanding of authority that underscores his faith. He explains that, like a military officer who issues commands that are obeyed, he believes Jesus possesses an authority that transcends physical presence. He expresses confidence that Jesus merely speaking the word will be enough to heal his servant. This profound expression of faith astonishes Jesus, who commends the centurion for his belief, declaring it greater than any he has found in Israel, emphasizing faith's power regardless of one's background.

With the centurion's faith acknowledged, Jesus declares that the servant will be healed, and indeed, at that very moment, the healing occurs. This miracle is significant, illustrating not only Jesus' divine authority over illness but also affirming the centurion's insight into spiritual authority. The servant's healing underscores a broader message of the Gospel: faith in Jesus transcends cultural and religious boundaries, offering grace and transformation to all who believe. This encounter serves as a powerful testament to the inclusive reach of Jesus' ministry, celebrating a faith demonstrated through trust in his word and resulting in miraculous outcomes.

Jesus Heals a Paralytic

In Capernaum, word spreads quickly that Jesus has returned home, drawing a large crowd to the house where he is staying. The gathering is so dense that there is no room left, not even outside the door, as people eagerly listen to his teaching. Amidst this scene, four friends arrive, carrying a paralyzed man on a mat. Their determination to see their friend healed is evident as they find themselves unable to reach Jesus through the packed entrance, illustrating both their desperation and faith in Jesus' ability to heal.

Undeterred by the obstacles, the friends hatch an unconventional plan. They make their way to the roof of the house, creating an opening through which they lower the paralyzed man directly in front of Jesus. This act of creative persistence demonstrates their unwavering belief in Jesus' power and their deep love for their friend. Jesus, seeing their faith, addresses the paralyzed man with unexpected words: "Son, your sins are forgiven." This pronouncement shocks some of the teachers of the law present, who silently question Jesus' authority to forgive sins, believing it to be blasphemy.

Aware of their doubts, Jesus addresses the challenge by posing a question: is it easier to say "Your sins are forgiven" or "Get up, take your mat, and walk"? To validate his authority on earth to forgive sins, Jesus commands the paralyzed man to rise, take his mat, and walk. Immediately, the man stands up, his paralysis cured, and walks out in full view of the amazed crowd. This dual healing of body and spirit not only confirms Jesus' divine authority but also leaves the witnesses glorifying God, exclaiming they had never seen anything like it. This event reinforces the extent of Jesus' authority, encompassing both physical healing and spiritual forgiveness, and highlights the power of faith and persistent hope.

Jesus Heals Man with Withered Hand

As Jesus continues his ministry, he enters a synagogue on the Sabbath, where he encounters a man with a withered hand. The Pharisees, constantly scrutinizing Jesus' actions, seize this moment as an opportunity to challenge him, hoping to accuse him of breaking Sabbath laws. They pose a question, asking whether it is lawful to heal on the Sabbath, seeking to trap Jesus between compassion and strict religious observance. This setting reflects the ongoing tension between Jesus and the religious authorities, who prioritize legalism over mercy.

Jesus addresses their challenge with a question of his own, using a practical analogy. He asks them if they would rescue a sheep fallen into a pit on the Sabbath, emphasizing the value of compassion and human need over rigid adherence to the law. By stating that humans are far more valuable than sheep, he underscores the importance of doing good regardless of the day, thereby advocating a deeper understanding of the Sabbath's purpose. This response not only highlights the inconsistency in their thinking but also shifts the focus from legalism to the heart of God's law — love and mercy.

Without waiting for further debate, Jesus instructs the man to stretch out his hand, and upon doing so, the hand is completely restored. This miraculous healing serves as a powerful demonstration of Jesus' authority and compassion. Rather than celebrating the healing, the Pharisees react with hostility, conspiring to plot against Jesus for undermining their authority. This encounter highlights the growing opposition Jesus faces as he challenges traditional interpretations of the law, advocating instead for a compassionate and merciful approach that reflects God's true intentions.

Jesus Raises a Widow's Son from the Dead

As Jesus travels to the town of Nain, he is accompanied by his disciples and a large crowd, eager to witness his teachings and miracles. Upon approaching the town gate, they encounter a somber scene: a funeral procession for the only son of a grieving widow. The loss of her son not only plunges the widow into profound sorrow but also leaves her vulnerable in a society where widows without male support face significant hardship. The large crowd accompanying her underscores the community's shared mourning and the gravity of her plight.

Moved by compassion, Jesus approaches the widow and gently tells her not to weep. His empathy and authority prompt him to intervene in the unfolding tragedy. He touches the bier, halting the procession, and speaks directly to the dead young man, commanding, "Young man, I say to you, get up." Instantly, the young man sits up and begins to speak, a miraculous restoration of life that astonishes all who witness it. This act of raising the dead highlights Jesus' unparalleled power over life and death, revealing his divine authority and deep compassion for human suffering.

The crowd is filled with awe and reverence, recognizing the miracle as a profound sign of God's presence among them. They glorify God, acknowledging Jesus as a great prophet and declaring that God has come to help his people. The news of this remarkable event spreads throughout Judea and the surrounding regions, amplifying Jesus' reputation and ministry. This narrative not only demonstrates Jesus' compassion and authority but also underscores the hope and restoration he brings, affirming his mission to restore life and offer comfort to the brokenhearted.

Jesus Calms the Storm

As Jesus and his disciples set out across the Sea of Galilee in a boat, an intense storm arises, with winds and waves threatening to capsize their vessel. The disciples, experienced fishermen familiar with the sea, find themselves frightened by the ferocity of the storm, highlighting the severity of their situation. Amidst the chaos and panic, Jesus remarkably remains asleep, undisturbed by the tumult around him. This juxtaposition between Jesus' calm and the disciples' fear sets the stage for a profound lesson in faith and divine authority.

Driven by their desperation and fear for their lives, the disciples wake Jesus, pleading for his help and expressing their fear of perishing. Jesus, upon waking, addresses their fear and lack of faith, questioning why they are so afraid despite his presence with them. He stands and rebukes the winds and the sea with authority, and immediately, there is a great calm. The sudden cessation of the storm leaves the disciples in awe, prompting them to marvel at the nature of the man who can command even the winds and the waves, and they obey.

This event underscores Jesus' divine authority over nature, reinforcing his identity as more than just a teacher or prophet. The disciples are faced with the reality of his power, compelling them to reflect on their faith and understanding of who Jesus is. It also highlights the transformative power of faith amidst fear, illustrating the peace and assurance found in trusting Jesus' presence and authority. This miracle serves as a powerful reminder of Jesus' sovereignty and the importance of faith, encouraging believers to trust in his power and presence despite life's storms.

Jesus Casts Demons into a Herd of Pigs

As Jesus arrives on the eastern shore of the Sea of Galilee in the region of the Gadarenes, he is immediately confronted by two men possessed by demons. These men emerge from the tombs, a place of isolation and despair, reflecting their tormented state. Their condition is so severe that they are considered dangerous, and people avoid passing that way. The presence of the demons in the men fills the atmosphere with an oppressive tension, setting the stage for a dramatic encounter between the forces of darkness and the authority of Jesus.

Upon seeing Jesus, the demons within the men recognize his divine authority, crying out, "What do you want with us, Son of God? Have you come here to torture us before the appointed time?" Their reaction underscores Jesus' identity and power, even acknowledged by the spiritual realm. Nearby, a large herd of pigs is feeding, and the demons beg Jesus to send them into the pigs if he drives them out. Granting their request, Jesus commands them to go, and the demons exit the men and enter the pigs, which then rush down the steep bank and perish in the water.

This powerful act of deliverance not only liberates the men from their torment but also demonstrates Jesus' unmatched authority over evil forces. The townspeople, however, respond with fear rather than faith when the herders report what happened. Confronted with the magnitude of the miracle and the loss of their livestock, they plead with Jesus to leave their region. This encounter highlights both the liberation that Jesus brings to those in bondage and the varied human responses to his transformative power—ranging from awe and gratitude to fear and rejection.

Jesus Heals a Woman in the Crowd

As Jesus makes his way through a bustling crowd, a woman who has been suffering from bleeding for twelve years quietly approaches him from behind. Her condition has left her not only physically weakened but also socially and religiously isolated, as she is considered unclean under Jewish law. Driven by desperation and faith, she believes that simply touching the edge of Jesus' cloak will heal her. Her discreet attempt reflects both her hope and her fear of drawing attention in a society that marginalizes her condition.

Upon touching Jesus' cloak, the woman instantly feels relief as her bleeding stops, signifying that her faith has led to her healing. Although she intended to remain unnoticed, Jesus perceives that healing power has gone out from him. Turning to see her, he addresses her directly, reassuring her with kindness and affirming her faith. He says, "Take heart, daughter, your faith has healed you," emphasizing the transformative power of belief and acknowledging her as part of the community with the tender address of "daughter."

This encounter between Jesus and the woman with the issue of blood highlights the personal nature of faith and healing. It illustrates how faith, even in its most humble and quiet expression, can lead to profound transformation and restoration. By addressing her publicly, Jesus not only heals her physical ailment but also restores her dignity and status within the community. This narrative reinforces the theme of Jesus' compassion and the power of faith, providing hope to those who might feel marginalized or isolated in their struggles.

Jesus Raises Jairus' Daughter Back to Life

As Jesus returns from the region of the Gerasenes, he is greeted by a welcoming crowd who have been eagerly awaiting his arrival. The enthusiasm of the people underscores his growing reputation as a healer and teacher, drawing individuals from various walks of life who seek his wisdom and miracles. Amidst this crowd, a prominent figure emerges—Jairus, a synagogue leader. His position in the community is one of respect and authority, yet at this moment, he is simply a desperate father in dire need.

Jairus approaches Jesus with humility and urgency, falling at his feet and pleading for him to come to his house. His only daughter, who is about twelve years old, is gravely ill and near death. The plea of Jairus is both a testament to his faith in Jesus' power to heal, as well as to his desperation as a parent fighting for the life of his child. Despite his status, Jairus casts aside any social and religious conventions that might deter him, focusing solely on his daughter's well-being.

Moved by Jairus's earnest request, Jesus sets out with him toward his home, accompanied by the pressing crowd. The throng of people underscores the challenge of their journey and the public nature of the unfolding events. This narrative moment creates a palpable tension as it sets the stage for subsequent acts of faith and divine intervention. Within the broader context of the crowd's anticipation, Jairus's personal story highlights the intersecting themes of faith, desperation, and Jesus's willingness to respond to those in need, regardless of their social standing.

Jesus Heals Two Blind Men

As Jesus departs from a previous encounter, he is followed by two blind men who cry out persistently, "Have mercy on us, Son of David!" Their plea signifies both their desperation and their recognition of Jesus as the promised Messiah, a testament to their faith despite their physical inability to see. Their use of the title "Son of David" highlights their belief in Jesus' messianic identity and power to heal, setting the stage for a profound demonstration of faith.

Jesus continues walking until he reaches a house, where the blind men manage to follow him indoors, demonstrating both their determination and faith in his ability to heal them. Once inside, Jesus questions them, asking if they truly believe that he can restore their sight. Their affirmative response further underscores their unwavering faith, despite the challenges posed by their blindness. Jesus, moved by their conviction, touches their eyes and declares that their faith has made healing possible, and their sight is immediately restored.

After their healing, Jesus instructs the men to keep the miracle private, yet their profound gratitude and the magnitude of the event make silence difficult. They spread the news of their healing throughout the region, inadvertently expanding Jesus' reputation and influence. This narrative emphasizes the power of faith in receiving healing and the personal nature of Jesus' miracles, demonstrating his compassion for those genuinely seeking his help. Moreover, it illustrates the tension between Jesus' instructions for discretion and the natural human response to share life-altering experiences.

Jesus Heals a Man Who Was Unable to Speak

As Jesus continues his ministry, a mute man possessed by a demon is brought before him. The man's inability to speak is both a physical ailment and a spiritual bondage, illustrating the intertwining of spiritual and physical realms in the Gospel narratives. Those who bring the man to Jesus do so with faith, trusting in his reputation and power to heal. This act of bringing the man to Jesus demonstrates the community's role in seeking healing and restoration on behalf of those unable to advocate for themselves.

Upon encountering the mute man, Jesus casts out the demon, and immediately the man regains his ability to speak. This miraculous healing elicits amazement from the crowd, who marvel at the unprecedented nature of Jesus' works, saying nothing like this has ever been seen in Israel. The healing not only restores the man's voice but also signifies the broader liberation Jesus offers from spiritual oppression. The crowd's reaction underscores the recognition of divine intervention in Jesus' actions, heightening his growing impact and the spread of his fame.

However, not everyone is convinced of the benevolence behind Jesus' miracles. The Pharisees, witnessing the same event, claim that Jesus drives out demons by the prince of demons, attempting to undermine his authority and mission. This accusation illustrates the growing opposition and skepticism Jesus faces from religious leaders threatened by his influence. The stark contrast in reactions—from amazement to accusations—highlights the division in perceptions of Jesus' identity and the disruptive nature of his ministry, which challenges established religious norms and power structures.

Jesus Heals an Invalid at Bethesda

In Jerusalem near the Sheep Gate, lies a pool called Bethesda,known for its supposed healing properties. The area is crowded with a multitude of disabled individuals—blind, lame, and paralyzed—hoping for a miraculous cure. Among them is a man who has been paralyzed for thirty-eight years, embodying a longstanding struggle and a life defined by dependency and helplessness. His situation depicts a profound sense of waiting, highlighting the human longing for healing and change.

Jesus approaches this man with a question that seems simple yet profound: "Do you want to get well?" The man explains his predicament, expressing his inability to reach the pool in time during the stirring of the waters, as he has no one to help him. This response reveals both his desire and resignation, a cycle seemingly unbroken over decades. Jesus, bypassing the need for the pool, commands him, "Get up! Pick up your mat and walk," and immediately, the man is healed. His ability to stand and walk marks a transformative moment, not just physically but symbolically as well, moving from hope deferred to immediate restoration.

Later, when Jesus encounters him in the temple, he advises him to "stop sinning or something worse may happen to you," linking physical healing with spiritual well-being. The man, now aware of who healed him, informs the Jewish leaders, which escalates their growing animosity toward Jesus. This healing act on the Sabbath stirs controversy, focusing the leaders' ire on Jesus' perceived disregard for Sabbath laws. The event encapsulates the theme of Jesus' authority over traditional practices and his transformative impact on personal lives, while also foreshadowing the mounting conflict between Jesus and religious authorities.

Jesus Feeds the Five Thousand

Upon hearing the news of John the Baptist's death, Jesus withdraws by boat to a solitary place, seeking solace and reflection. Despite his desire for solitude, the crowds, moved by their need and drawn by his presence, anticipate his destination and follow him on foot from the surrounding towns. As Jesus steps ashore, he is greeted by a vast multitude, and moved by deep compassion, he begins to heal their sick, setting aside his own weariness to address the pressing needs before him. This reveals his profound empathy and unwavering commitment to his mission of service.

As evening approaches, the disciples, concerned about the remote location and the lateness of the hour, urge Jesus to send the crowd away to buy food. However, Jesus challenges them, saying, "You give them something to eat," inviting them to trust in divine provision. When they respond by highlighting their meager resources—only five loaves and two fish—Jesus instructs the crowd to sit down on the grass. He takes the loaves and fish, looks up to heaven, gives thanks, and breaks the loaves, demonstrating a profound act of faith and reliance on God's abundance.

Miraculously, the disciples distribute the food, and not only does it suffice, but everyone eats until satisfied. Remarkably, twelve baskets of leftovers are collected, one for each disciple, symbolizing divine providence and abundance. This miracle of feeding about five thousand men, besides women and children, underscores Jesus' authority over the natural order and illustrates the principle of abundance from scarcity through faith. The event also foreshadows the spiritual nourishment Jesus offers, inviting believers into a deeper understanding of reliance and trust in God's provision.

Jesus Walks on Water

Following the miraculous feeding of the five thousand, Jesus instructs his disciples to get into a boat and go ahead of him to the other side of the Sea of Galilee while he dismisses the crowd. Seeking solitude and connection with the Father, he then ascends a mountainside to pray. As night falls, the disciples find themselves far from land, struggling against strong winds and rough seas, illustrating the physical and metaphorical challenges they face without Jesus' immediate presence.

In the early hours before dawn, Jesus approaches the boat, walking on the water, an astounding display of his divine authority over nature. The disciples, terrified and thinking he is a ghost, cry out in fear. Jesus immediately reassures them with his presence and voice, saying, "Take courage! It is I. Don't be afraid." Encouraged by Jesus' words, Peter boldly asks to join him on the water. Jesus invites him to come, and Peter begins to walk towards him, demonstrating a moment of remarkable faith.

However, as Peter focuses on the wind and waves, his initial faith wavers, and he begins to sink. Crying out for salvation, Jesus immediately reaches out, catches him, and gently admonishes his lack of faith. They both climb into the boat, and the wind dies down, bringing calm and relief to the disciples. Overwhelmed by the events, the disciples worship Jesus, proclaiming, "Truly you are the Son of God." This episode deepens their understanding of Jesus' divine nature and emphasizes the power of faith, illustrating both the challenges of doubt and the reassurance found in Jesus' steadfast presence.

Jesus Heals the Sick in Gennesaret

After calming the storm and astonishing his disciples with his divine power, Jesus and his followers arrive at the region of Gennesaret. Word of his arrival quickly spreads throughout the area, as the people recognize him and his reputation for miraculous healings. Eager to witness his transformative power, the locals start bringing all those who are ill from surrounding towns and villages to wherever Jesus may be found. This immediate gathering underscores the anticipation and hope of encountering the healing presence of Jesus.

The sick and their families, driven by faith, believe that simply touching the fringe of Jesus' garment will suffice for healing. This belief highlights the profound faith and desperation of the people, who are willing to reach out even for the smallest contact with Jesus' cloak. Their willingness to trust in his power to heal reflects the deep impact Jesus has had on those who have previously witnessed or heard about his miracles. The landscape of Gennesaret becomes a testament to faith as people gather around him.

As individuals reach out and touch his garment, they experience immediate healing, affirming the divine power and compassion of Jesus. Each miraculous recovery serves as a testament not only to Jesus' authority but also to the power of faith itself. Those who experience healing praise Jesus, reinforcing his role as a divine healer capable of transforming lives. Through these acts, the narrative emphasizes the boundless grace available to those who seek Jesus with belief, illustrating the profound impact of faith and the embodiment of hope and restoration found in his presence.

Jesus Heals Woman's Demon-Possessed Daughter

In the region of Tyre and Sidon, Jesus encounters a Canaanite woman who approaches him with a desperate plea. Her daughter is tormented by a demon, and she cries out to Jesus for mercy, addressing him as "Lord, Son of David." This title acknowledges Jesus' messianic identity, showing her recognition of his authority and power despite being a Gentile. The woman's approach reflects both her desperation as a mother and her deep belief in Jesus' ability to heal.

Initially, Jesus responds with silence, and his disciples urge him to send the woman away. When he finally speaks, he explains that his mission is to the lost sheep of Israel. Undeterred, the woman kneels before him, imploring, "Lord, help me!" Jesus responds with a metaphor about children's bread not being tossed to the dogs, reflecting the prioritization of his mission. However, the woman cleverly turns the metaphor to her advantage, asserting that even dogs eat the crumbs that fall from their masters' table.

Impressed by her persistent faith, Jesus acknowledges the greatness of her belief and grants her request. Her daughter is healed at that very moment, demonstrating the power of unwavering faith and illustrating the inclusive nature of Jesus' mercy. This encounter not only underscores the universal reach of Jesus' compassion but also highlights the transformative power of faith, which transcends cultural and religious boundaries. The Canaanite woman's story becomes a profound testament to the belief that faith, combined with humility and persistence, can lead to divine intervention and healing.

Jesus Heals a Deaf and Mute Man

As Jesus continues his journey, he travels through the region of the Decapolis, eventually arriving in a predominantly Gentile area. There, people bring to him a man who is deaf and has a speech impediment. Seeking Jesus' healing touch, they implore him to place his hand on the man. This scene reflects the growing recognition of Jesus' reputation as a healer among diverse communities, highlighting the widespread hope he inspires among those suffering from various ailments.

Taking the man aside from the crowd to ensure a personal and intimate encounter, Jesus performs a series of actions that connect with the man's physical senses. He puts his fingers into the man's ears and, after spitting, touches the man's tongue. Looking up to heaven, Jesus sighs deeply and commands, "Ephphatha," which means "Be opened." Immediately, the man's ears are opened, and his tongue is loosened, enabling him to hear and speak clearly. This physical and spiritual healing underscores Jesus' compassion and his ability to communicate across barriers of silence and isolation.

Despite urging the people not to tell anyone, the witnesses of the miracle cannot contain their astonishment and joy. They proclaim Jesus' deeds widely, overwhelmed by his power to make the deaf hear and the mute speak. This narrative not only highlights Jesus' miraculous abilities but also emphasizes the transformative impact of his ministry, which brings healing and openness to those isolated from their communities. The spreading of this news speaks to the profound impression Jesus leaves on all who witness his acts of compassion and power, reinforcing the theme of hope and restoration that defines his mission.

Jesus Feeds the Four Thousand

In the midst of a large gathering, Jesus finds himself surrounded by a crowd that has been with him for three days, captivated by his teachings. The people, having exhausted their food supplies, are now in a remote area without access to nourishment. Out of compassion for the crowd and concerned for their well-being, Jesus expresses to his disciples the need to provide them with something to eat, fearing that some might faint on their journey home if sent away hungry. This concern sets the stage for another demonstration of his miraculous provision.

The disciples, aware of the scarcity of resources, question how they could possibly feed such a large multitude in such a desolate place. Jesus inquires about the quantity of bread available, to which they respond with seven loaves. Taking the loaves, Jesus gives thanks, breaks them, and hands them to his disciples to distribute to the people. Along with a few small fish, which he also blesses, the food is distributed, and everyone eats and is satisfied. Remarkably, seven basketfuls of leftovers are collected, underscoring the abundance generated from scarcity.

Following this miraculous feeding of about four thousand people, Jesus dismisses the crowd and then gets into a boat with his disciples, crossing to the region of Dalmanutha. There, he is confronted by the Pharisees, who demand a sign from heaven to test him. Despite the miraculous feeding they were previously aware of, their skepticism persists. Jesus, deeply sighing, responds that no sign will be given to this generation. This interaction highlights the tension between Jesus' demonstrated compassion and power and the persistent disbelief of some religious leaders, emphasizing themes of faith and the blindness of those who demand proof despite evident miracles.

Jesus Heals a Blind Man at Bethsaida

When Jesus arrives at Bethsaida, a town with a reputation for skepticism, he is met by people bringing a blind man, imploring Jesus to heal him. Their plea reflects a growing recognition—despite the town's reputation—of Jesus' ability to perform miracles. The scene sets the stage for a unique demonstration of Jesus' healing process, highlighting both physical and spiritual dimensions.

Taking the blind man by the hand, Jesus leads him outside the village, choosing a private setting for this encounter. He uses spit to moisten the man's eyes, then lays his hands on him and asks if he can see anything. The man's initial response is partial sight; he sees people, but they appear to him like walking trees, suggesting an incomplete healing. This gradual process is distinctive, signifying a layered approach to healing that involves both physical restoration and the growth of faith.

Jesus places his hands on the man's eyes once more, prompting a complete restoration of sight. The man's vision is made clear, symbolizing both literal and metaphorical clarity. After the healing, Jesus instructs him not to return to the village, emphasizing the personal nature of this miracle. This healing narrative not only showcases Jesus' compassion and power but also serves as a metaphor for spiritual insight and the gradual journey toward full understanding and faith. Through this encounter, the layered process of healing becomes a reflection of the deeper truth that spiritual enlightenment often unfolds gradually.

Jesus Heals a Man Born Blind

As Jesus walks through Jerusalem, he encounters a man who has been blind from birth. His disciples, curious about the cause of the man's condition, ask whether it is due to his own sin or that of his parents. This question reflects a common belief of the time—that personal afflictions are the result of sin. Jesus, however, reframes the situation, stating that the man's blindness is an opportunity to reveal the works of God, emphasizing that suffering can serve a divine purpose and lead to greater understanding and belief.

To heal the man, Jesus performs a unique miracle. He spits on the ground, creates mud with the saliva, and applies it to the man's eyes. Jesus then instructs him to wash in the Pool of Siloam. The man follows these instructions, and upon washing, he miraculously gains sight for the first time in his life. This act not only restores the man's physical sight but also symbolizes the spiritual enlightenment that comes from faith and obedience to Jesus' word. The transformation highlights Jesus' role as the light of the world and brings into focus the broader theme of seeing beyond physical sight.

Following the healing, the man returns, stirring confusion and amazement among his neighbors and those who have known him as a blind beggar. They debate his identity, some questioning whether he is the same man, while others affirm the miracle they witness. The man himself confirms the transformation and recounts his encounter with Jesus. This testimony initiates a ripple effect, encouraging those who hear it to question and search for understanding, illustrating how personal testimony can inspire faith and provoke curiosity about Jesus' true nature. The story invites reflection on the themes of perception, belief, and the transformative power of divine intervention.

Jesus Heals a Demon-Possessed Boy

Upon descending from the mountain after the Transfiguration, Jesus encounters a tumultuous scene where a distraught father approaches him, kneeling and pleading for his son. The boy is severely afflicted by seizures, often falling into fire or water, making his condition life-threatening. The father explains that he had brought his son to the disciples, but they were unable to heal him. This inability highlights a moment of weakness in the disciples' faith and sets the stage for Jesus to demonstrate his authority and power.

Jesus expresses frustration with the faithless and perverse generation, lamenting their lack of belief. Nonetheless, he instructs for the boy to be brought to him. With a command, Jesus rebukes the demon, and it immediately leaves the boy, who is healed from that moment. This miraculous healing underscores Jesus' divine authority and compassion, showcasing his ability to restore where others could not. The event serves as a powerful testament to Jesus' mastery over spiritual and physical ailments.

Later, in private, the disciples inquire why they were unable to cast out the demon. Jesus explains that their failure stems from their insufficient faith, emphasizing, "If you have faith as small as a mustard seed, you can say to this mountain, 'Move from here to there,' and it will move." This teaching illustrates the profound potential of genuine faith, even if it appears small. Jesus' words encourage the disciples to cultivate a deeper trust and confidence in God's power, highlighting the limitless possibilities when faith is present. The narrative serves as a poignant reminder of the vital connection between faith and divine intervention.

The Temple Tax

When Jesus and his disciples arrive in Capernaum, tax collectors approach Peter with a query regarding the temple tax, a tribute required annually from Jewish males for temple upkeep. They inquire whether Jesus, as a teacher and leader, pays this tax. Peter, acknowledging their concern, affirms that Jesus does indeed pay it. This interaction underscores the societal and religious expectations of the time, reflecting the careful scrutiny under which Jesus and his disciples operated.

Later, as they gather in a house, Jesus anticipates Peter's thoughts about the tax. He initiates a conversation by asking whether kings collect taxes from their own children or from others. Peter responds that taxes are collected from others, to which Jesus concludes that the children are exempt. This dialogue highlights Jesus' identity as the Son of God, implying his exemption from the tax meant for God's temple, yet it also underscores his wisdom in addressing earthly obligations.

To avoid causing offense, Jesus instructs Peter to go to the lake, cast a line, and take the first fish he catches. Inside the fish's mouth, Peter finds a coin exactly sufficient to cover the tax for both Jesus and himself. This miracle subtly reveals Jesus' divine knowledge and authority over creation, providing a practical resolution that upholds social harmony. It demonstrates how Jesus navigates between fulfilling spiritual truths while respecting societal customs, teaching a lesson in humility, obedience, and the pragmatic application of faith.

Jesus and Beelzebul

As Jesus continues his ministry, he encounters a man possessed by a demon that has rendered him mute. Demonstrating his divine authority, Jesus casts out the demon, and immediately the man regains his ability to speak. This miraculous healing astounds the crowd, leaving them in awe and wonder at the power and compassion Jesus embodies. The restoration of the man's speech serves as a testament to Jesus' role in bringing liberation and clarity to those bound by spiritual and physical ailments.

Despite the miraculous display, some onlookers remain skeptical and accuse Jesus of driving out demons by the power of Beelzebul, the prince of demons. Their accusations reflect a refusal to acknowledge the divine nature of Jesus' authority and are rooted in disbelief and opposition. Others, eager for further validation, demand additional signs from heaven. In response, Jesus addresses their skepticism by emphasizing the absurdity of their claim, explaining that a kingdom divided against itself cannot stand, and if Satan were to drive out his own forces, his kingdom would inevitably fall.

To further clarify, Jesus asserts that if he casts out demons by the finger of God, it signifies the arrival of God's kingdom. He illustrates his point with a parable about a strong man guarding his possessions, only to be overpowered by one stronger. Here, Jesus portrays himself as the stronger force overcoming the devil's hold. Concluding with a stark message, Jesus declares that those who are not with him are against him, emphasizing the need for decisiveness in faith. This narrative highlights the tension between recognizing divine authority and the resistance faced by those who choose disbelief, underscoring the importance of unity and allegiance in the spiritual battle.

Jesus Heals Woman Crippled for 18 years

While teaching in a synagogue on the Sabbath, Jesus notices a woman who has been crippled for eighteen years, bent over and unable to stand upright due to an afflicting spirit. Her condition has not only impacted her physically but also signifies the social and spiritual burdens she carries. Moved by compassion, Jesus calls her forward during the service, embodying his willingness to heal and restore amidst rigid religious customs. His attention to her plight highlights his profound empathy and his mission to bring freedom to those oppressed.

As she approaches, Jesus declares her free from her ailment and lays his hands on her. Immediately, the woman stands up straight, experiencing liberation and wholeness for the first time in nearly two decades, prompting her to glorify God. This miraculous healing on the Sabbath showcases Jesus' authority over the constraints of illness and his prioritization of mercy and compassion over strict adherence to Sabbath laws. Her instant transformation serves as a testament to the power and immediacy of Jesus' healing presence, which transcends traditional limitations.

However, the synagogue leader becomes indignant, citing the Sabbath law that restricts work on this holy day and urging that healings should occur on the other six days of the week. Addressing this, Jesus responds by calling out the hypocrisy in their mindset, pointing out that they would untie and water their animals on the Sabbath, so why should this woman, a "daughter of Abraham," not be freed from her bondage on such a day? His argument silences his opponents and shames them, while the crowd rejoices at the wondrous acts he performs. This narrative not only highlights Jesus' challenge to legalistic interpretations of the Sabbath but also underscores the broader theme of liberation and the joyous reception of divine compassion.

Jesus Heals a Man on the Sabbath

While teaching in a synagogue on the Sabbath, Jesus notices a woman who has been crippled for eighteen years, bent over and unable to stand upright due to an afflicting spirit. Her condition has not only impacted her physically but also signifies the social and spiritual burdens she carries. Moved by compassion, Jesus calls her forward during the service, embodying his willingness to heal and restore amidst rigid religious customs. His attention to her plight highlights his profound empathy and his mission to bring freedom to those oppressed.

As she approaches, Jesus declares her free from her ailment and lays his hands on her. Immediately, the woman stands up straight, experiencing liberation and wholeness for the first time in nearly two decades, prompting her to glorify God. This miraculous healing on the Sabbath showcases Jesus' authority over the constraints of illness and his prioritization of mercy and compassion over strict adherence to Sabbath laws. Her instant transformation serves as a testament to the power and immediacy of Jesus' healing presence, which transcends traditional limitations.

However, the synagogue leader becomes indignant, citing the Sabbath law that restricts work on this holy day and urging that healings should occur on the other six days of the week. Addressing this, Jesus responds by calling out the hypocrisy in their mindset, pointing out that they would untie and water their animals on the Sabbath, so why should this woman, a "daughter of Abraham," not be freed from her bondage on such a day? His argument silences his opponents and shames them, while the crowd rejoices at the wondrous acts he performs. This narrative not only highlights Jesus' challenge to legalistic interpretations of the Sabbath but also underscores the broader theme of liberation and the joyous reception of divine compassion.

Jesus Heals Ten Men With Leprosy

As Jesus journeys toward Jerusalem, he travels along the border between Samaria and Galilee, a region known for its complex social and ethnic tensions. Along his path, he encounters ten men afflicted with leprosy, a disease that renders them social outcasts and unclean according to Jewish law. Standing at a distance, as custom dictates, they raise their voices, pleading for Jesus to have mercy on them. This collective cry reflects their hope and belief in his power to heal despite their marginalized status.

In response, Jesus instructs the ten lepers to go and show themselves to the priests, following the law that requires a priestly declaration for a healed leper to be reintegrated into society. As they proceed, they are miraculously cleansed of their leprosy. The act of healing, occurring as they move in faith toward the priests, reinforces themes of obedience and trust in Jesus' word. However, only one of the ten, realizing his healing, returns to Jesus, praising God with a loud voice. Notably, this man is a Samaritan, highlighting the inclusive nature of Jesus' ministry.

Upon his return, the Samaritan leper falls at Jesus' feet in gratitude, an act of deep humility and recognition of Jesus' divine role. Jesus acknowledges the man's faith, but also questions the absence of the other nine, underscoring a significant point about gratitude and acknowledgment. He tells the Samaritan, "Rise and go; your faith has made you well." This moment emphasizes that spiritual healing and salvation transcend physical healing, and that true faith is demonstrated through gratitude and recognition of God's work in one's life. The narrative highlights the universal scope of Jesus' ministry and the profound importance of faith and gratitude.

Jesus Raises Lazarus from the Dead

In the village of Bethany, Mary and Martha send word to Jesus that their brother Lazarus is gravely ill. Despite his love for the family, Jesus deliberately remains where he is for two more days, hinting to his disciples that this illness will lead to God's glory and not end in death. This decision sets the stage for a profound demonstration of Jesus' power over life and death. Eventually, Jesus announces that Lazarus has died and expresses his intention to awaken him, which the disciples misunderstand as literal sleep.

Upon arriving in Bethany, Jesus is met by Martha, who expresses both her grief and faith, saying that if Jesus had been there earlier, her brother wouldn't have died. Jesus reassures her with the promise of resurrection, and Martha affirms her belief in the final resurrection at the last day. Jesus makes a profound declaration that he is the resurrection and the life, inviting Martha to deepen her faith in his divine identity. Meanwhile, Mary also comes to Jesus, weeping, and he is deeply moved by the sorrow of Mary and the mourners, leading him to weep as well—showing his deep compassion and humanity.

Approaching the tomb, Jesus orders the stone to be removed despite Martha's concern about the odor, reminding her of the need to believe to see God's glory. After offering a prayer of thanksgiving and calling out loudly, "Lazarus, come out," Lazarus emerges from the tomb, still bound in grave clothes. Jesus instructs the bystanders to unbind him, completing the miracle and restoring Lazarus to life. This powerful act causes many witnesses to believe in Jesus, cementing his role as one who wields divine authority over death. The narrative underscores the themes of faith, the revelation of Jesus' divine nature, and the foreshadowing of his own resurrection.

Blind Bartimaeus Receives His Sight

As Jesus makes his way through Jericho, accompanied by a large crowd, a blind beggar named Bartimaeus sits by the roadside. Despite his lack of sight, Bartimaeus is keenly aware of the commotion and inquires about its cause. Upon learning that Jesus of Nazareth is passing by, he seizes the moment and cries out loudly, "Jesus, Son of David, have mercy on me!" This title, "Son of David," reflects Bartimaeus's recognition of Jesus' messianic identity and highlights his faith despite his marginalized status.

The crowd, attempting to maintain order, rebukes Bartimaeus, urging him to be quiet. However, his determination only grows stronger, and he calls out even more fervently. Jesus, hearing his cry, stops and instructs the crowd to call Bartimaeus to him. Their tone shifts as they inform the beggar that Jesus is calling for him. Encouraged, Bartimaeus throws aside his cloak, a sign of his eagerness and faith, and makes his way to Jesus, demonstrating his deep trust and hope for transformation.

When Bartimaeus reaches Jesus, he is asked, "What do you want me to do for you?" Without hesitation, Bartimaeus requests his sight be restored. Jesus acknowledges his faith, declaring, "Go, your faith has healed you." Immediately, Bartimaeus regains his sight and follows Jesus along the road, joining the throng of disciples and onlookers. This encounter not only illustrates the power of persistent faith but also highlights the openness and compassion of Jesus, who is receptive to the cries of those in need. The narrative underscores the transformative power of faith and the enduring hope that accompanies belief in Jesus' healing touch.

The Withered Fig Tree

As Jesus returns to the city from Bethany early in the morning, he experiences hunger along the way. Spotting a fig tree by the roadside, he approaches it only to find that it bears no fruit, just leaves. In response, Jesus speaks a curse upon the tree: "May you never bear fruit again!" Instantly, the fig tree withers, demonstrating the power of his word and authority. This unexpected action becomes a visual parable for the disciples, illustrating deeper spiritual lessons beyond the mere incident.

The disciples, observing the rapid withering of the tree, are amazed and perplexed by the suddenness of the change. Their amazement prompts them to question Jesus about how the fig tree withered so quickly. Jesus uses this moment to teach them about the nature of faith and prayer, emphasizing that faith without doubt can accomplish great deeds. He assures them that not only can they perform acts like withering a fig tree, but they can also move mountains if they believe without wavering.

Jesus further reinforces the lesson by highlighting the power of prayer, instructing that whatever they ask for in prayer, as long as they hold firm belief, will be granted. This teaching challenges the disciples to cultivate a faith that is active and bold, capable of trusting in God's power to bring about change. Through the withered fig tree, Jesus conveys the importance of authentic faith and the potential it unlocks in the believers' lives, urging them to rely on prayer and unwavering belief as they continue their spiritual journey.

Jesus Heals a Servant's Severed Ear

In the tense and shadowed moment of Jesus' arrest in the Garden of Gethsemane, the atmosphere crackles with urgency and conflict. A crowd, led by Judas Iscariot, approaches Jesus, equipped with swords and clubs, sent by the chief priests and elders. As they step forward to seize Jesus, one of his disciples, moved by a surge of defensive loyalty, reacts impulsively by drawing his sword. In a swift attempt to protect Jesus, the disciple strikes the servant of the high priest, slicing off his right ear. This reaction encapsulates the confusion and fear gripping Jesus' followers as they witness the unfolding betrayal.

In stark contrast to this violent act, Jesus responds with calm authority and compassion. He immediately intervenes, telling his disciples to cease their resistance, indicating a transcendent understanding of the events at hand. Then, in a profound act of mercy that echoes his teachings on loving one's enemies, Jesus touches the servant's ear and miraculously heals him. This healing amidst chaos serves as a testament to Jesus' unwavering commitment to peace and restoration, even for those who come as his adversaries.

By healing the servant, Jesus provides a profound illustration of his mission to bring reconciliation rather than retribution. The act draws a sharp line between the ways of violence and the divine path of mercy, offering a powerful, tangible lesson to his disciples and the crowd. In a moment where hostility could have escalated, Jesus' healing serves as a transformative gesture, reminding all present—and future generations—of the boundless compassion that defines his ministry, even at the cusp of his own suffering and sacrifice.

The Second Miraculous Catch of Fish

At dawn, as soft light begins to emerge over the Sea of Galilee, the disciples are returning from a long night of fruitless fishing. Unaware of the significance of the figure on the shore, they hear a voice calling out to them, inquiring about their catch. The man on the shore, who is Jesus but unrecognized by the disciples, suggests they cast their net on the right side of the boat. Though weary and skeptical, the disciples follow the stranger's advice, leading to an astonishing and overwhelming haul of fish, more abundant than they could have anticipated.

As the net fills to bursting, the disciple whom Jesus loved perceives the figure's true identity, exclaiming to Peter, "It is the Lord!" Struck with the realization, Peter, in his typical fervency, immediately girds himself and plunges into the sea, eager to reach Jesus with an urgency that underscores his devotion and longing for reconciliation. Meanwhile, the other disciples remain with the boat, towing the net laden with fish, their hearts lifted by the familiar and miraculous presence of their risen Lord.

Upon reaching the shore, the disciples find Jesus beside a fire, where fish and bread are already being prepared for breakfast. The haul is counted to reveal 153 large fish, yet despite the number, the net remains miraculously intact. This abundant catch, reminiscent of their initial calling, symbolizes renewal and preparation for their continuing mission. The scene is laden with themes of recognition, provision, and the sustaining presence of Jesus, who provides not only physical sustenance but also spiritual renewal, ushering his disciples into a deeper understanding of their calling in the wake of his resurrection.

For any inquiries or further information, please do not hesitate to reach out to us at info@shoebill.com

www.ingramcontent.com/pod-product-compliance
Lightning Source LLC
Chambersburg PA
CBHW050452110426
42744CB00013B/1972